THE FUNNIEST SCOTLAND QUOTES... EVER!

Also available

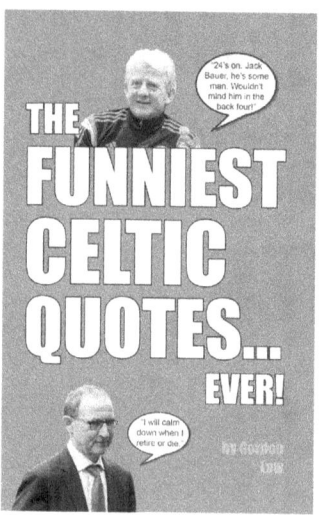
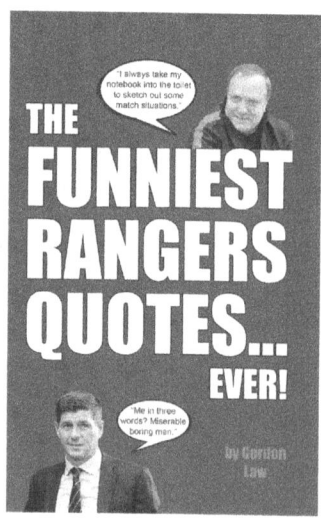

The Funniest Liverpool Quotes... Ever!

The Funniest Chelsea Quotes... Ever!

The Funniest Spurs Quotes... Ever!

The Funniest Arsenal Quotes... Ever!

The Funniest Man City Quotes... Ever!

The Funniest Newcastle Quotes... Ever!

The Funniest United Quotes... Ever!

The Funniest Everton Quotes... Ever!

THE FUNNIEST FOOTBALL QUOTES.... EVER!

"If they made a film of my life, I think they should get George Clooney to play me."

"Mario woke up this morning with a hardening – in his thigh!"

by Gordon Law

Copyright © 2020 by Eagle Books.

No part of this publication may be reproduced, stored in a retrieval system or transmitted in any form by any means, electronic, mechanical, photocopying, or otherwise, without prior written permission of the publisher Eagle Books.

contact@gmediagroup.co.uk

Printed in Europe and the USA
ISBN: 978-1-917744-23-2
Imprint: Eagle Books

Photos courtesy of: Tomasz Bidermann/Shutterstock.com; Featureflash Photo Agency/Shutterstock.com

Contents

Introduction..6

Calling The Shots...9

Talking Balls...15

Call The Manager..21

Sweet FA..27

Game For a Laugh...33

Media Circus..47

Off The Pitch..53

Field of Dreams...61

Managing Just Fine..69

Pundit Paradise...85

Fan Fever..95

Introduction

Scotland may have yet to win a major tournament, but the team is amongst the best in the world at providing entertaining characters.

There's never a dull moment off the pitch as the national side's managers have treated us to an endless array of hilarious sound bites.

Gordon Strachan is never short of something to say and is renowned for his sarcastic one-liners and withering put-downs. Whether it's blaming genetics for failing to qualify for the World Cup or blasting a reporter for asking a stupid question, Strachan is always good value.

The long-serving Craig Brown had a brilliant sense of humour and came out with a series of strange musings and memorable muck-ups while he was in charge.

Jock Stein had a huge impact on Scottish football and the charismatic boss will also be remembered for his witty statements.

"The secret of being a good manager is to keep the six players who hate you away from the five who are undecided," was one of his pearls of wisdom.

Former striker Ally McCoist always has a comedic quip, Alan Rough loves an amusing anecdote, while fellow keeper Andy Goram never minces his words.

Many more rants and ramblings can be found in this unique collection of funny Scotland quotes and I hope you laugh as much reading this book as I did in compiling it.

Gordon Law

THE FUNNIEST SCOTLAND QUOTES... EVER!

CALLING THE SHOTS

THE FUNNIEST SCOTLAND QUOTES... EVER!

"We asked Maurice Johnstone who his ideal room mate on a Scotland trip would be and his sheet came back with 'a big blonde' written on it."
Craig Brown

"You're from Drumchapel, laddie. What do you know about prawn cocktails? You'll have a soup like the rest of us."
Jock Stein to Andy Gray on an away trip

"Craig Beattie's an important player for us. He's quick, he's very fast, and he's got great pace."
Alex McLeish

Calling The Shots

"He has what I call that lunatic mentality, and I mean that in a good way. He was like Scott Brown at Celtic. It gets cold in Glasgow you know, but those two would walk around with just their t-shirts on."
Gordon Strachan on Kieran Tierney

"At his age, he is not going to play forever."
George Burley on David Weir

Andy Roxburgh: "My touch has gone. I'll need to take a couple of weeks to get it back."
Unknown player: "It'll need to be a couple of weeks in Lourdes."

THE FUNNIEST SCOTLAND QUOTES... EVER!

"John Spencer's hamstring is making alarm bells ring in my head."

Craig Brown

"Don't thank me, it was my wife. I was sitting at the table and I said I needed another goalie. She said, 'I like that Alan Rough'. So you were in."

Jock Stein to Alan Rough after recalling him to the squad in 1985

"You would have thought I had murdered one of their next of kin."

Craig Brown on the reaction to dropping Paul McStay from the squad

Calling The Shots

"Barry Ferguson and Nigel Quashie can play in any team in the world."
Berti Vogts

"They were unavailable to us the last time, we're unavailable to them this time. Their ability has nothing to do with this."
Andy Roxburgh on Steve Nicol and Gary Gillespie being omitted from the squad

"He used to talk, talk, talk about how wonderful he was. I said, 'Look, Spenny, you've had two visits to the toilet at Hampden and you think you're a footballer, so shut up'."
Craig Brown on John Spencer

THE FUNNIEST SCOTLAND QUOTES... EVER!

TALKING BALLS

THE FUNNIEST SCOTLAND QUOTES... EVER!

"Joe Jordan takes his teeth out and is a nasty b*stard on the park. But off the park, if you were in a pub, you'd find him sitting in a corner drinking half a lager and lime, quiet as a lamb."
Kenny Burns on his Scotland teammate

"If he was a chocolate drop, he'd eat himself."
Archie Gemmill on Graeme Souness

"Dick Dastardly had a miserable time [touring with Scotland] in the USA but we suspect he was missing Muttley."
Ally McCoist on Darren Jackson

Talking Balls

"He used to nick my bacon sandwiches. I was always hungry and I was always eating garbage. He used to hijack my food. He would sit down near the bar of our hotel and watch for room service coming. He'd ask the waiter, 'Where are they going? Mr Strachan ordered them? No son, they're for me now'. I used to ring up and say, 'Where's my sandwiches?'. They'd say, 'Mr Stein had them'."

Gordon Strachan on Jock Stein

"I remember trying to light this thing in the bloody room to keep insects away but I think Robbo got bitten all over his a*se. Right enough, it was some size of an a*se."

Kenny Burns on John Robertson

THE FUNNIEST SCOTLAND QUOTES... EVER!

"Jim Baxter drove him mad calling him Jimmy Clitheroe but Bally couldn't get near enough to him to do anything about it."

Billy Bremner compares Alan Ball to the high-pitched comedian Jimmy Clitheroe

"He took part in a move we were rehearsing and, after his first touch, he shouted across to Andy Roxburgh who was the boss at the time. 'Sair tae' he yelled and walked off. 'Sair tae' in English translates into 'sore toe'. But rather than call the physio on or say to Andy what was happening, he just shouted across and disappeared."

Gary McAllister on Duncan Ferguson training with Scotland for the first time

Talking Balls

"They caused a moment of panic when one of them went down in training with a spot."
Ally McCoist on Eoin Jess and Scott Booth

"When he got up in the morning, he would lift his legs over the bed, put his feet down and he'd go straight into his socks, shoes, trousers, shirt, tie, everything and pull everything up, like a big zip. That's Robbo."
Kenny Burns on John Robertson

"The only man in the Scotland squad who could walk on to the back of a horse."
Ally McCoist on Jim Leighton

THE FUNNIEST SCOTLAND QUOTES... EVER!

CALL THE MANAGER

THE FUNNIEST SCOTLAND QUOTES... EVER!

"I strongly feel that the only difference between the two teams were the goals that England scored."

Craig Brown on the Euro 96 game

"The bottom line is [Peter] Beardsley comes from God."

Andy Roxburgh after the England striker's winner in 1988

"There is no denying the better team won, but we had a great chance not to lose."

Craig Brown after his team lost 2-1 to Brazil

Call The Manager

"The ball hit a water sprinkler and shot high into the air. It was purely an instinctive reaction when Richard Gough grabbed the ball as it flew over his head."

Andy Roxburgh defends his player after he saw red against Switzerland

"When [Ally McCoist] broke his leg against Portugal, he was lying on the table with his leg in a splint and someone said, 'How are you feeling?'. He says, 'It could be worse, we could have lost 5-0'."

Craig Brown had to tell him Scotland were in fact defeated 5-0

THE FUNNIEST SCOTLAND QUOTES... EVER!

"The worst player scored from a cross by the second worst."

Ally MacLeod after England's Steve Coppell converted a Peter Barnes cross to deny Scotland victory

"He'd score 99 times out of 100 and unfortunately this was the one occasion he didn't."

George Burley on Chris Iwelumo's terrible miss against Norway

"They had a dozen corners, maybe 12 – I'm guessing."

Craig Brown

Call The Manager

"Guys, I've just seen Brazil holding hands. They're sh*tting themselves!"

Craig Brown after seeing 1998 World Cup opponents Brazil linking arms in the tunnel

"They wouldn't have been able to score a 'lucky' goal if they hadn't been in our six-yard box."

Craig Brown on losing to Brazil

"We don't have a Kenny Dalglish or Denis Law anymore. In Germany we call it – like the nice Beatles record – yesterday. It was yesterday."

Bertie Vogts after playing the Faroe Islands

THE FUNNIEST SCOTLAND QUOTES... EVER!

SWEET FA

THE FUNNIEST SCOTLAND QUOTES... EVER!

"When new people get involved in clubs we ask them to pop down and have a chat. They are amazed that we do not have three heads and actually look like them."

Scottish FA chief executive Jim Farry

"Given the job I have, you can't be laugh-a-minute Jim or the karaoke king of the SFA."

Jim Farry

"I didn't appoint Berti Vogts. I recommended him to the executive committee and they appointed him. And that's not me trying to get off the hook."

SFA chief executive David Taylor

Sweet FA

"The girls in our office at the SFA have nicknames for us all. Frank Coulston is Old Spice and Ross Mathie is Grey Spice because of his hair. I hate to admit this but I'm Constipated Spice. At my age I spend more time in the loo than the rest. I tell them it's because I'm the only one who washes his hands."

Craig Brown

"All I ever read is criticism of Jim Farry. For some reason the fact that he was a market gardener is held against him. He joined my staff at the SFA when he was 16 years old so I don't know when he fitted in gardening. But is there something wrong with gardening?"

Former SFA secretary Ernie Walker

THE FUNNIEST SCOTLAND QUOTES... EVER!

"It is interesting to me to read that I 'growl' or 'roar' or 'fume'. I don't. I just speak."
Jim Farry

"The subtleties of our language were maybe a little beyond him."
SFA president John McBeth after manager Craig Brown quit

"We do our best to ensure that when we come into contact with people they leave saying, 'Hey, you're not like the guy I read about'. Now all I need to do is meet another 4.9 million people and the job's easy."
Jim Farry

Sweet FA

"I consider myself one of the best administrators in Europe but there has been criticism directed towards me which has abused the platform that journalists have for comment."

Jim Farry

"I'm a gregarious guy and I can tell and take a joke."

Jim Farry

"What kind of person do we need? I would say Superman."

SFA president Jack McGinn after Jim Farry's departure

THE FUNNIEST SCOTLAND QUOTES... EVER!

GAME FOR A LAUGH

THE FUNNIEST SCOTLAND QUOTES... EVER!

Q: "What's the biggest improvement to have taken place in Scottish football in the last 10 years?"

A: "The standard of the sweet trolleys at Scotland national team get-togethers. More used by Craig Brown than any of the players, though."

Pat Nevin

"It's a big regret for me, not playing for Scotland, but I look at some of the people who have been capped and you realise if they give out caps that cheaply, maybe I'm better off without one."

Rangers' John Brown

Game For a Laugh

"To be a keeper you've got to be strong mentally because if you make a mistake it often ends up in the back of the net."

Jordan Archer

"The reason why I'm a Liverpool player is the same reason why I'm captain of my country: I've worked my b*llocks off to get where I am."

Andy Robertson

"Our qualifying campaign was a successful failure."

Kenny Miller on Scotland trying to make it to Euro 2008

THE FUNNIEST SCOTLAND QUOTES... EVER!

"Once you retire, you retire."

Andy Goram on quitting the national team

"Some people want me to return to the Scotland squad but it will never happen."

Andy Goram

"There was never any thought in my mind that I did not want to play for Scotland ever again."

Andy Goram the very next day

"The competition was treated almost as an end-of-season tour."

Neil Mochan on the 1954 World Cup

"Players from other countries have always told me they're taken aback, because when they're on the pitch, Scottish or English footballers never shut up."

Colin Hendry

"This is not a reality check for us because we never thought we were Brazil."

Christian Dailly on the defeat to Belarus

"If patriotism is silly, then OK, we're silly. When we go on to the field for Scotland, we're ready to give blood. Of course, we'd like a lot of money, but even without it we'll play till we drop."

David Hay at the 1974 World Cup

THE FUNNIEST SCOTLAND QUOTES... EVER!

"Players don't want sympathy from their peers at a time like this. They want to be the butt of the squad's jokes because, believe it or not, it helps."

Jim Leighton on joining up with Scotland after he was dropped by Man United for the 1990 FA Cup Final replay

"I'd like to thank several people. First of all Bob Wilson for giving me encouragement when I needed it most. After all, someone with two caps ought to know what he's talking about."

Alan Rough takes a swipe after Wilson criticised his performances

Game For a Laugh

"Jocks love to beat England. Forget the World Cup, European finals, for Scottish fans, beating England is everything. It's a history thing, simple as that. Go back centuries, to the battles of Bannockburn, Falkirk or Culloden."

Alan Hansen

"I much prefer 'Flower of Scotland' to 'Scotland The Brave' as our pre-match anthem... I'm told 'Flower' can be a bit politically insensitive – sending the English homeward to think again – but that doesn't stop Princess Anne belting it out every rugby international."

Gary McAllister

THE FUNNIEST SCOTLAND QUOTES... EVER!

"I don't know if Alex McLeish knows whether I'm Scottish or not. Maybe I'll have to put 'Mac' in front of my surname."
Chris Iwelumo

"We looked like Liquorice Allsorts."
Willie Fernie on Scotland's 1954 World Cup players who trained in their own kit

"All the Scotland posters in my room had been ripped down after the games against Peru and Iran. After that goal [Archie Gemmill's against Holland] they went back up."
Gary McAllister recalls the 1978 World Cup

"We respect them for the good players that they are but at the end of the day if you have to kick them, you kick them."

Kenny Miller reveals Scotland's tactics

"I just kept my head down. There was so much sh*t flying around."

Graeme Souness on the 1978 World Cup

"What reputation do Holland have anyway? They didn't qualify for the last World Cup and they're in the play-offs, so it's not a great record, is it?"

James McFadden before Scotland lost 6-1 in their two-legged play-off with the Dutch

THE FUNNIEST SCOTLAND QUOTES... EVER!

"The simplest solution is to stop the ball getting to Ronaldo in the first place. If the ball does get to him, we have to make sure he has no space to turn or knock the ball into. And if that doesn't work, we'll have to tie his shoelaces together."

John Collins on Scotland's plans for Brazil at the 1998 World Cup

"I was the only British player to play 450 games and never get a red or yellow card. That could even be a world record for a defender. Speed is all I had. No one could run past me. I couldn't tackle a fish supper."

Eric Caldow

Game For a Laugh

"It should go back to one generation – otherwise you get into that Irish thing of having a pint of Guinness and you can play."

Former Scotland star Richard Gough on George Boyd representing Scotland after his grandfather was born in Motherwell

"A lot of fuss was made, and even more nonsense written, after Scotland fans dug up some Wembley turf in June 1977. The pitch was about to be ripped up anyway – the Tartan Army just began the job a few days early."

Kenny Dalglish

THE FUNNIEST SCOTLAND QUOTES... EVER!

"Unless we batter sides, we are on a hiding. The way international football is going that won't happen very often. Yet if we don't play well and win, we're rubbish. And if we play well and don't win, we're rubbish."
Christian Dailly

"Whenever I play in London, I always get Seaman rammed down my throat."
Gary McAllister on being taunted by the England fans after his Euro 96 penalty miss

"I don't get up or down about it because I didn't do anything wrong."
Willie Johnston on the 1978 World Cup

Game For a Laugh

"I now know why Rod Stewart and Sean Connery don't stay in Scotland. You can't get any peace. We're sitting ducks."

Andy Goram after pulling out of Scotland's World Cup squad

"I've never met this woman and I never will."

Gary McAllister on the England team's faith healer Eileen Drewery offering to help him recover from a knee injury

"I remember the game because I managed to do something very few players can claim – I set up an international goal for Brian McClair!"

Ally McCoist recalls his 50th cap

THE FUNNIEST SCOTLAND QUOTES... EVER!

MEDIA CIRCUS

"Oh, no, no, no, no. I'm not going to sit here and answer questions from members of the public. They can do it themselves. You think it's a hotline here? It's like I'm on Radio Clyde on a Saturday night. For goodness sake! No, you're not getting any now because they're coming for other people. You'll have to think about your own ones. Right, anybody else?"

Gordon Strachan tells a journalist he doesn't want questions from fans

"If people had seen me walking on water, you can be sure someone, somewhere would have complained, 'Look at that Berti Vogts, he can't even swim'."

Berti Vogts on criticism from the media

Media Circus

"You won't have to go down to get quotes from the players... the supporters will bring them up in a minute."

Ally MacLeod to journalists after their 1977 win when Scotland fans invaded the pitch

Brazilian reporter: "What do you think of Brazil?"

Kenny Dalglish: "I think he's a great player."

The forward at the 1982 World Cup

"Tell Rodney to get a f*cking move on! Or I'm off! Where's Rodney?"

Gordon Strachan gets agitated with a Maltese interviewer while waiting to go live

THE FUNNIEST SCOTLAND QUOTES... EVER!

"You can mark down 25th June, 1978, as the day Scottish football conquers the world."
Ally MacLeod's boast to the media before Scotland's first-round World Cup exit

Brazilian journalist: "Do you dream about Ronaldo?"
Colin Hendry: "I'm a happily married man with three children. I don't dream about other men."

"You get headlines saying 'Fans in Rage at Brown', but I haven't met an angry one yet. They usually say, 'It was the best three weeks of my life'."
Craig Brown on the 1998 World Cup

Media Circus

Reporter: "What would you do if you win the World Cup?"

Ally MacLeod: "Retain it."

The manager at the 1978 tournament

"I'd say if the Scottish press corps took on the Italian press corps on their knowledge of football, our lads would get a terrible beating. The Italians are far superior in the reading and scrutiny of what's happening."

SFA chief executive Jim Farry

"Concorde has arrived!"

Ally MacLeod on being unveiled as the new manager, touching the side of his nose

THE FUNNIEST SCOTLAND QUOTES... EVER!

OFF THE PITCH

THE FUNNIEST SCOTLAND QUOTES... EVER!

"I once gave the Scotland players the afternoon off in Athens. One asked where there was to go. The hotel porter suggested the Acropolis and one of the lads said, 'I didn't know the discos were open in the afternoon'."

Craig Brown

"He was better than Ally McCoist."

Andy Roxburgh after hearing Ferenc Puskas sing at a coach's course

"I hate sunbathing. I think it's the biggest waste of time imaginable."

Craig Brown

Off The Pitch

"Players are no worse now than they were 30 years ago. It's getting to a stage where players will have to carry a contract in their pockets for girls to sign, saying that they consent to sex and won't go running to the papers."

Peter Lorimer, who once revealed he and seven players from the Scotland squad had sex with a woman during the World Cup

"I thought she was outstanding. Lovely girl. When she came on she was wearing no jewellery at all. No earrings, no necklace, no rings whatsoever. And I thought, 'That's class'."

Craig Brown on meeting Kylie Minogue on Ally McCoist's chat show

"I now have a farm in Lanark. I've got two pygmy goats – Gin and Tonic."

Andy Goram

"I was quite upset. Everyone knows Jock is bald and ugly."

Craig Brown on getting mixed up with his TV commentator brother

"I was in Moldova airport and I went into the duty-free shop – and there wasn't a duty-free shop."

Andy Gray

Off The Pitch

"[Rod Stewart] embarrasses me by calling me, 'Mr Brown, can I join in with training?'"

Craig Brown

"Don't shoot, I'm the goalkeeper!"

Alan Rough to armed guards while climbing a wall to get into his hotel after being locked out at the World Cup in Argentina

"I can walk on my hands around a penalty box. It was something I learned when I was a PE teacher."

Craig Brown

THE FUNNIEST SCOTLAND QUOTES... EVER!

"Some of the younger players think that lager makes you invisible."

Craig Brown

"I don't know why I'm the only one that gets labelled with it because a lot of people had one. I seem to be the only one that people remember."

Alan Rough on his memorable perm hairstyle at the 1978 World Cup

"I reckon his suit cost more than my house."

Craig Brown on appearing on TV with Glenn Hoddle

Off The Pitch

"My brother Bob has three degrees from universities, my other brother Jock has an MA from Cambridge and I've got a BA from the Open University. As a player I was the one the manager would turn to last and say, 'Right son, nothing clever from you this week'."

Craig Brown

"I can remember taking my seat in the stand at Hampden before a Scotland game and being picked out by a spectator who was obviously not a Celtic supporter. 'McGrain, ya Fenian b*stard!' he shouted up at me before realising that was not accurate. He then shouted, 'Ya diabetic b*stard!'. I had to laugh."

Danny McGrain, who was a diabetic

THE FUNNIEST SCOTLAND QUOTES... EVER!

FIELD OF DREAMS

THE FUNNIEST SCOTLAND QUOTES... EVER!

"Roy Aitken told Mo Johnston to spit at Glenn Hysen's feet in the tunnel. Mo said he'd probably trap it and ply it up the park."
Andy Goram after a World Cup clash with Sweden

"I remember wondering how he'd react to a good physical challenge. I never got within a yard of him."
Graeme Souness on Zico

"Diving f*cking cheats."
Christian Dailly after Scotland lose to Germany following a controversial penalty

Field Of Dreams

"I can tell Celtic fans he has one of the nicest a*ses in football – I should know because I spent all day chasing it around the park."
Darren Jackson on Rivaldo's back side in the 1998 World Cup

"Everywhere I went people would shout at me, 'What time is it, Frank? Nine past Haffey'."
Frank Haffey on Scotland's 9-3 defeat to England in 1961

"I haven't had a good night's sleep since that game and it's more than 40 years ago."
Frank Haffey continues

THE FUNNIEST SCOTLAND QUOTES... EVER!

"I remember swapping jerseys with Franco Baresi. What was depressing was that he got a sweat-soaked Scotland No.9 shirt while the Italy No.6 I got in return was not only bone-dry but still smelling of his cologne."

Ally McCoist

"I think I'd have booed as well if I was sitting there watching it."

James McFadden after a 3-0 Hungary loss

"They could've thrown a kitchen sink into the box and one of the guys would've headed it."

Paul Lambert on the meeting with Holland

Field Of Dreams

"I was going to score an own goal, just to say I'd got a hat-trick at Wembley. Then Denis Law, who had played in the 9-3 game, told me that he would kill me if I did that."

Jim Baxter netted Scotland's goals in the 1962 win over England

"I remember leading up to the game. [Edgar] Davids and [Clarence] Seedorf had said, 'We don't know any of their players' and I think coming off the pitch there were one or two of our players going, 'Well, you know us now!'."

Colin Hendry after frustrating Holland at Euro 96

"If he had said anything to me after the game I would have punched him."

Andy Goram after Paul Gascoigne's strike in Euro 96

"Are you not ashamed to be on the same pitch as me?"

Jim Baxter to England's Alan Ball in 1967

"I was confident, put my foot out and it hit the heel. I'm gutted but I'll take that one on the chin."

Chris Iwelumo on missing that open goal against Norway

Field Of Dreams

"I've watched it again but my missus made me delete it after about five days."

Chris Iwelumo erases his embarrassing miss against the Norwegians

"It got him out of jail really, because he had a cr*p championship."

Colin Hendry on Paul Gascoigne's Euro 96 goal against Scotland

"You get plenty of slaps in the face in this game and it's fair to say this is one of them."

Jim Leighton after losing to Morocco at the 1998 World Cup

THE FUNNIEST SCOTLAND QUOTES... EVER!

MANAGING JUST FINE

THE FUNNIEST SCOTLAND QUOTES... EVER!

"Hagi is a brilliant player, but we're not going to get psychedelic over him."

Andy Roxburgh ahead of the Romania game

"Can you believe my luck? Scotland get to the World Cup Finals and the guy in charge wears a wig and has a nose that could cut a wedding cake."

Scotland No.2 Craig Brown on manager Andy Roxburgh

"I've told the lads this is a rehearsal for the World Cup final."

Ally MacLeod when Scotland played Brazil in a friendly before the tournament

Managing Just Fine

"In the last campaign we were the second smallest, apart from Spain. We had to pick a team to combat the height and strength at set-plays. Genetically we have to work at things, maybe we get big women and men together and see what we can do."

Gordon Strachan

"I don't dislike the English, I hate their guts!"

Ally MacLeod before Scotland's visit to Wembley

"The easiest team for a manager to pick is Hindsight XI."

Craig Brown

THE FUNNIEST SCOTLAND QUOTES... EVER!

"It's a Dutch invention but we started it in Scotland."

Andy Roxburgh

"I've done everything in my career, but this will be something new and different."

Terry Butcher on becoming Scotland coach

"We do have the greatest fans in the world, but I've never seen a fan score a goal."

Jock Stein

Q: "Your high point as Scotland manager?"
Craig Levein: "When I got the sack."

Managing Just Fine

"If I was to declare an interest in this job the Tartan Army would string me up."

Alex McLeish says he doesn't want the vacant Birmingham City position

"Zidane and Vieira? They're only names. I think we can win this game."

Berti Vogts ahead of Scotland's 5-0 defeat to France in his first game as boss

"If you have any intelligence then you get stick. You're supposed to be rough and tough and one of the lads."

Craig Brown on footballers

THE FUNNIEST SCOTLAND QUOTES... EVER!

"Football management these days is like nuclear war. No winners, just survivors."

Tommy Docherty

"Old Firm supporters went to internationals to cheer three players, boo two, and ignore the rest!"

Jock Stein on Scotland fans

"Roll up your sleeves and get f*cked in. The skill will take care of itself."

Willie Ormond, who ended every team talk with this message to the players

Managing Just Fine

"At Euro 92, there were calls for McCoist to be dropped from the team. Someone, in protest, put a giant poster under my door. Under the photo of Ally there was the message, 'Please don't drop me, Andy' and signed, 'The Golden Slipper' (he was the Golden Boot winner). I still don't know who was responsible."

Andy Roxburgh

"We are not a big footballing nation any more. I'd love to watch my players in games between Manchester United and Arsenal, but instead I have to travel to see Bristol City versus Wigan."

Berti Vogts

THE FUNNIEST SCOTLAND QUOTES... EVER!

"Get stuck into the f*cking Germans."

The very German Berti Vogts to the Scotland players before a World Cup qualifier

"Bagpipes, warpaint and claymores won't win us games in the European Championship or World Cup."

Craig Brown at Euro 96

"Remember I've seen a video tape of a Scotland v England match and I've seen him miss a chance from five yards. It was against England and he couldn't score. So what does that say?"

Berti Vogts responds to criticism from Charlie Nicholas

Managing Just Fine

"Kevin [Keegan] and I have 63 international caps between us. He has 63 of them."

Craig Brown

"I'd have preferred it if neither England nor West Germany had reached the final in 1966. I'm not a great lover of the Germans – they bombed my folks' house in Clydebank in the war."

Ally MacLeod

"It was good to see them train and get a feel of them."

George Burley

THE FUNNIEST SCOTLAND QUOTES... EVER!

"I think I'm 4-1 to get a red card in the tunnel – it would be the fist of Terry Butcher rather than the hand. While we will never forget, it's not about that game. I haven't got a Maradona doll that I stick pins in every day, I don't need psychiatric help."

Scotland coach Terry Butcher on facing new Argentina boss Diego Maradona

"He is a big boy now and he has to grow up and move on!"

George Burley wants Butcher to get over it

"I'm going to a country where I'm adored!"

Diego Maradona on his first game in charge

Managing Just Fine

"Our guys are getting murdered twice a week."
Andy Roxburgh on the number of domestic fixtures

"To watch the BBC Sports Review of the Year, you'd have thought that England would have won the tournament if only [David] Beckham had stayed on the pitch."
Craig Brown on World Cup 98

"We were at Dundee United together in our younger days and were similar types of player – cr*p."
Walter Smith on his old pal Dick Campbell, the Partick Thistle manager

THE FUNNIEST SCOTLAND QUOTES... EVER!

"I am Scotland manager until something else happens."

Alex McLeish

"With a bit of luck in the World Cup I might have been knighted. Now I'll probably be beheaded."

Ally MacLeod after Scotland's 1978 exit

"If a kid sees me getting into my car at a game he'll ask for my autograph and then more of them will turn up. But I know there's always one at the back saying, 'Who is he anyway?'"

Craig Brown

Managing Just Fine

"Pressure to me is being homeless or unemployed. This isn't pressure, it's pleasure."

Andy Roxburgh after 17 of his players pulled out of the squad

"Charisma comes from results, and not vice versa."

Craig Brown

"I think it's going to take three or four years to see how important the work of Berti Vogts was in Scotland."

Only one person could have said this – Berti Vogts

THE FUNNIEST SCOTLAND QUOTES... EVER!

"If I was a punter I'd rather have Kenny Dalglish too."

Craig Brown on talk that Scotland should have chosen a big-name manager

"The secret of being a good manager is to keep the six players who hate you away from the five who are undecided."

Jock Stein

"My job is my holiday. I travel all the time and see the world in this business. I take my holidays at home in Ayr."

Craig Brown

Managing Just Fine

"I know that feeling, when you're described to everybody as an idiot."

Berti Vogts

"My name is Ally MacLeod and I am a winner."

The manager introduces himself to the Scotland squad

"I used to be a raving lunatic as a club manager."

Craig Brown

"The first year was torture."

Andy Roxburgh on being Scotland boss

THE FUNNIEST SCOTLAND QUOTES... EVER!

PUNDIT PARADISE

THE FUNNIEST SCOTLAND QUOTES... EVER!

"The Scots have really got their hands cut out tonight."
Trevor Francis

"I'm not convinced that Scotland will play a typically English game."
Gareth Southgate

"I don't think what he wanted to do got across to some players. And also I think some of them are too thick to take it on board – and not good enough to take it on board anyway, to be perfectly honest with you."
Craig Burley on ex-Scotland manager and uncle George Burley

"Scotland don't have to score tonight, but they do have to win."

Billy McNeill

"He's a big lad. If he said it was Christmas you'd sing carols."

Ian St John on Matt Elliott

"We've given the lad some stick for diving but since then he's come on leaps and bounds."

Billy Dodds

"The Tartan Army can be our tenth man tomorrow."

Alan Rough on Holland versus Scotland

THE FUNNIEST SCOTLAND QUOTES... EVER!

"A performance as flat as Kate Moss's chest."

Pat Nevin after Scotland's 1998 World Cup defeat to Morocco

Barry Davies: "Oh, look at that, between his legs!"

David Pleat: "Beautiful, isn't it?"

Commentary during Scotland v Morocco

"I think Walter [Smith] will be on the phone to the Samaritans."

Charlie Nicholas on Scotland's draw for the Euro qualifiers

Pundit Paradise

"We'll be home before the postcards."

Tommy Docherty after Scotland drew Brazil, Norway and Morocco in the 1998 World Cup

"Aye, and so was Tommy."

Craig Brown's reply, referring to Docherty's 1954 World Cup campaign

"Chris Iwelumo's open-goal miss was the equivalent of falling out a plane and missing the Earth."

Chick Young on the striker's howler for Scotland against Norway

THE FUNNIEST SCOTLAND QUOTES... EVER!

"I don't want to sound homophobic but I want a Scottish manager."

Pat Nevin

"Scotland were like a dog with a bone and when they got the bone, they made it count."

Charlie Nicholas

"Some of the Scotland players need to look at themselves in the face."

Alan Brazil

"All the cul-de-sacs are closed for Scotland."

Joe Jordan

Pundit Paradise

"Today, if your granny was born in Dundee, you can play for Scotland. You shouldn't have these foreign lads all over the place, f*cking Nigel Squashie and all that lot. Christ, come on!"

Tommy Docherty gets Nigel Quashie's name totally wrong

"See ya. Daft little ground, silly game, f*ck off."

Richard Keys doesn't realise he is on air during pictures of Faroe Islands v Scotland

"James McFadden has been a Taliban for Scotland."

Charlie Nicholas

THE FUNNIEST SCOTLAND QUOTES... EVER!

"We've been playing against San Marino for an hour and it has just occurred to me that we're drawing 0-0 with a mountain top."
Ian Archer, radio pundit

"It looks like a night of disappointment for Scotland, brought to you live by ITV in association with National Power."
Brian Moore

"I'm a strong believer that if you score goals, you win matches."
Charlie Nicholas on George Burley's tenure

Pundit Paradise

"Scotland can't afford to take their minds off the gas."

Andy Townsend

"We Scots don't mind laughing at ourselves. But it's getting to the stage where other people are laughing at us."

Gordon Strachan

"I can't say England are sh*te because they beat us in the Euro 2000 play-offs, and that would make us sh*ttier."

Ally McCoist

THE FUNNIEST SCOTLAND QUOTES... EVER!

FAN FEVER

THE FUNNIEST SCOTLAND QUOTES... EVER!

"Deep-fry yer pizzas, we're gonna deep-fry yer pizzas."

Scotland supporters in Italy

"Deep-fry yer long boats, we're gonna deep-fry yer long boats."

The Tartan Army in Norway

"We hate Coca-Cola, we hate Fanta too, because we're the Tartan Army and we love Irn Bru!"

The fans can't get enough of the orange stuff

Fan Fever

"We're the famous Tartan Army and we're here to save the snail."

Scotland fans in Paris

"Bobby Moore, superstar, walks like a woman and he wears a bra."

Chant aimed at the England captain

"He's fat, he's round, he's kicked us out our ground. Robbie Williams, Robbie Williams."

The fan base come up with a witty song after the pop star's concert at Hampden Park forces them to Parkhead

THE FUNNIEST SCOTLAND QUOTES... EVER!

"Sing when you're whaling, you only sing when you're whaling!"

Scotland fans at the game with Iceland

"You can stick your f*cking chariots up your a*se!"

A chant aimed at the auld enemy

"Big f*cking pylon, it's just a big f*cking pylon!"

Mocking the Eiffel Tower in Paris

"Sing when you're fishing, you only sing when you're fishing. Sing when you're fishing!"

Another fishy song, this time to Norway

Fan Fever

"You put your left hand in, you put your left hand out. In out, in out and shake it all about. You do the Maradona and you turn around. That's what it's all about. Oooh Maradona, oooh Maradona, he put the English out, out, out."

Trolling England fans after the infamous 'Hand of God' moment at the 1986 World Cup

"We're gonna deep-fry your croissants!"

Scottish supporters in France

"What the hell is Va Va Voom?!"

The Tartan Army have another for the French

THE FUNNIEST SCOTLAND QUOTES... EVER!

"You're only half as good as last time!"

Scotland fans to Holland after conceding a third goal, having lost 6-0 previously

"We're representing Britain and we're gaunny do or die. England cannae dae it, cos they didnae qualify – hoy!"

The Scots enjoying themselves at the 1978 World Cup

"He's short, he's fat, he's gonna get the sack, Advocaat!"

Taunting the Holland manager after a 1-0 triumph

Fan Fever

"He's fat he's round, ideologically unsound. Kim Jong Il, Kim Jong Il..."

Supporters against Korea in the Kirin Cup

"Wembley, Wembley. Was the finest pitch in Europe till we took it all away. Wembley, Wembley..."

Remembering the 1977 pitch invasion in London

"One team in Tallinn, there's only one team in Tallinn."

Sang when Estonia failed to show up for the international

THE FUNNIEST SCOTLAND QUOTES... EVER!

www.ingramcontent.com/pod-product-compliance
Lightning Source LLC
Chambersburg PA
CBHW050303120526
44590CB00016B/2476